DO NOT REMOVE
CARDS FROM POCKET

6/94

OPRAH WINFREY

Television Star

by
Steve Otfinoski

A BLACKBIRCH PRESS BOOK

WOODBRIDGE, CONNECTICUT

Published by Blackbirch Press, Inc.
One Bradley Road, Suite 205
Woodbridge, CT 06525

©1993 Blackbirch Press, Inc.
First Edition

Manufactured in the United States

10 9 8 7 6 5 4 3 2 1

The publisher would like to thank Jeffrey Jacobs of Harpo Inc., for his valuable help in reviewing this manuscript.

Library of Congress Cataloging-in-Publication Data

Otfinoski, Steven.
    Oprah Winfrey: television star / by Steven Otfinoski.
       p.   cm. — (The Library of famous women)
    Includes bibliographical references and index.
    Summary: The life and career of the black talk show host who has become one of the most successful women in television.
    ISBN 1-56711-015-0 (lib. bdg.) ISBN 1-56711-061-4 (pbk.)
    1. Winfrey, Oprah—Juvenile literature. 2. Television personalities—United States—Biography—Juvenile literature. 3. Motion picture actors and actresses—United States—Biography—Juvenile literature. [1. Winfrey, Oprah. 2. Afro-Americans—Biography. 3. Television personalities. 4. Actors and actresses.] I. Title. II. Series.
PN1992.4.W56084 1993
791.45'028'092—dc20
[B]
93-21540
CIP
AC

Contents

Introduction

It was just another day of taping on the set of the tremendously popular daytime talk show, *The Oprah Winfrey Show.* The program's topic was, as it often is, a controversial one—incest. A guest was describing the terrible experience of being raped as a child by her father. The sensitive Oprah suddenly broke into tears and hugged the woman. This was not unusual. The talented young talk-show host is famous for her capacity to share in the feelings of her guests. What followed, however, was highly unusual.

Oprah signaled for a commercial break. When she came back a few minutes later, she shared the darkest secret of her life with millions of viewers. She revealed that she herself had been the victim of sexual abuse in her home from the ages of 9 to 14. It was a bombshell.

(*Opposite page*) Oprah Winfrey has achieved remarkable success as an actress, a producer, and a television talk-show host. *The Oprah Winfrey Show* was among the top five most-watched syndicated programs on television in 1992.

5

When the show ended, the switchboard lit up. The studio received thousands of calls. People told Oprah how much they admired her for her courage in speaking out. Many of them said that Oprah had given them the courage to talk about their own painful childhood abuse.

It is this kind of experience that has made Oprah Winfrey perhaps the most admired and popular woman in television today. She is much more than a talk-show host. She is a gifted actress and producer. She is an active supporter of causes she believes in. She gives funds generously to the needy. She gives her own time as a volunteer. Oprah has also become a role model. More important, she is a woman of honesty, compassion, and a great deal of courage. This is her story.

Chapter 1

Little Miss Misfit

Everything surrounding Oprah Winfrey's start in life was wrong—even her name. Oprah's parents had intended to name their daughter Orpah, after Ruth's sister-in-law in the Bible. But the midwife who delivered Oprah misspelled the name on the birth certificate. The midwife wrote down *Oprah* instead of *Orpah,* and *Oprah* is what the little girl was called.

Oprah was born on January 29, 1954, in Kosciusko, Mississippi—the result of a brief affair between Vernon Winfrey, a young soldier stationed at nearby Fort Rucker, and Vernita Lee, an 18-year-old farm girl.

A Gifted Child

Oprah's parents did not want to add to their already mounting mistakes, and so they didn't marry. Vernon was moved to another base. Vernita left baby Oprah in the care of her grandmother and headed north to find work as a domestic.

Life on her grandmother's farm was hard and lonely for little Oprah. There were no other children to play with or talk to, and her grandmother was a very stern woman. "She could whip me for days and never get tired," Oprah recalls with regret. Her only toy was a corncob doll; her only friends were the farm's pigs, chickens, and cows.

Oprah's imagination helped her cope. She talked to the cows while taking them to pasture and gave speeches to the pigs in their sty. Barely three, she gave her first public speech at the local church on the topic "Jesus rose on Easter Day." By the time Oprah was four, people were shaking their heads and saying, "That child is gifted."

Oprah knew she was special and wasn't afraid to say so. When she started kindergarten at the local school, she wrote this note to her teacher: "Dear Miss New. I do not think I belong here." Miss New agreed and immediately advanced her to the first grade. When the school year came to an end, Oprah was again skipped a year, to the third grade.

Oprah's life changed dramatically when the little girl turned six. For the next three

❋
By the time Oprah was four, people were shaking their heads and saying, "That child is gifted."

years, she was shuttled back and forth between her mother, who now lived in Milwaukee, Wisconsin, and her father, who had left the army and was currently living in Nashville, Tennessee.

By the time she was eight, Oprah was, in her own words, already a "champion speaker." Church groups and women's clubs listened in awe as the little girl made speeches, recited poetry, or gave dramatic readings. Oprah fondly recalled later, "Anybody needed anyone to speak any- thing, they'd call me."

At age nine, Oprah started living full-time with her mother. She joined Vernita Lee and her two half brothers in Milwaukee's black ghetto. Instead of farm animals, Oprah kept cockroaches in a jar as pets. Vernita Lee loved her daughter, but she was so busy trying to make a living as a domestic that she often didn't have enough time for Oprah. It was then that an event occurred that left emotional scars on Oprah for years to come.

Abused at Home

A teenaged cousin was baby-sitting with nine-year-old Oprah one afternoon at home and raped her. To calm her down afterwards, Oprah's cousin took her to the zoo. He bribed her to keep her mouth shut by buying her ice cream. But this was just the beginning of a pattern of abuse. Oprah was further sexually abused at home by an uncle and a trusted family friend. The abuse continued, off and on, until the young girl was 14.

"I didn't like making a big deal of it," Oprah recalls. "I really blamed myself for it, thinking something must be wrong with me." The feelings of guilt, shame, and low self-esteem she experienced are common symptoms of a sexually abused child.

Oprah felt awkward and uncomfortable at school. She desperately needed love, but she didn't think she was worthy of it. She would misbehave in extreme ways to get attention—attention she especially needed from her mother.

A Troubled Teenager

At age 13, Oprah decided that the way to become beautiful and popular was to buy a pair of octagon-shaped eyeglasses. Her mother explained that the family couldn't afford new glasses and that Oprah would have to make do with her old, ordinary glasses. Oprah reacted by waiting until she was all alone at home and breaking her glasses. Then she wrecked the apartment

to make it look as if a burglar had broken in. She also called the police.

"I decided to be unconscious when they came in and to have amnesia," she later recalled. Her distraught mother rushed to the hospital only to find Oprah moaning in a bed. One look at her daughter told Vernita that Oprah was faking. Of course Oprah made an extraordinary and

Oprah has shared her personal experience of abuse with the world in the hope that her story can help others. Here, Oprah makes an exit after testifying at a Senate Judiciary Committee hearing on child abuse in November 1991.

immediate "recovery." "She dragged me from the bed and we went home," she recalls. "Yes, I got the octagons."

But no pair of glasses could give the troubled teenager the self-confidence she so desperately needed. One day, Oprah saw famed soul singer Aretha Franklin on the street and told her a fantastic story about being abandoned in Milwaukee. Young Oprah was so convincing that the singer gave her $1,000 to get home. The girl took the money and got a room at a local hotel, where she lived it up for three whole days. A local minister found out where she was and dragged Oprah home to her mother.

Vernita Lee was beside herself. Oprah had become too much for a single mother to handle. Vernita tried to put her into a home for troubled girls, but it was filled. As a last resort, she sent Oprah to Nashville to live with her father, Vernon, and his wife. Vernita may not have known it at the time, but this was the best thing she could have done for her misfit of a daughter.

Chapter 2

From Beauty Queen to Anchorwoman

"My father saved my life," Oprah says today. "He simply knew what he wanted and expected. He would take nothing less." When Oprah first arrived in Nashville, Vernon Winfrey told his 15-year-old daughter, "You will not live in this house unless you abide by my rules."

Life with Father

Oprah's father had matured since his days in the army. He had married, settled down, and was a respectable member of the community in Nashville. Vernon ran a barber shop and was co-owner of a general store. He was a pillar of the local Baptist church. In 1975 he was even elected to the Nashville city council. Vernon got where he was by strict self-discipline. He used that same discipline on his wayward daughter.

Living with her father meant that Oprah had to make drastic changes in her lifestyle. She also had to apply herself in school. C's were no longer acceptable. Vernon knew his daughter's potential and wouldn't settle for anything less than her very best. Where the teacher's homework left off, his homework began. Oprah had to learn five new words every day, or there would be no dinner that night. She had to read a book every week and write a report on it. Television viewing was restricted to only one hour a day. Vernon was a tough taskmaster, but he was also a loving father. A stern look, he claimed, was all it took.

The discipline worked. Oprah's natural gifts were freed from the confusion and shame of her adolescence. She positively bloomed at Nashville's East High School. As one of the first African Americans at the school, Oprah made the honor list and was elected president of the student council. She excelled on the debating team and was a star in drama-club productions. At 16, she won a speech contest sponsored by the Elks Club. The prize was a full scholarship to Tennessee State University (TSU). But her public-speaking skills were about to take the talented teenager much farther than that.

A New Career

While trying to enlist sponsors for a March of Dimes walkathon, Oprah met John Heidelberg, a disc jockey at WVOL radio in Nashville. Heidelberg was so impressed by young Oprah's voice and self-confidence that he persuaded her to make an audition tape. Her skills were immediately apparent, and the station wasted no time in hiring her as a part-time announcer. She read the news after school and on weekends. Vernon Winfrey wasn't crazy about his daughter working at a radio station, but Heidelberg convinced him that Oprah had a talent worth nurturing.

WVOL helped open doors for Oprah in other ways as well. Each year Nashville's fire department held a beauty contest for Miss Fire Prevention. Local businesses chose employees to compete in the pageant. WVOL picked Oprah, who was quite trim and attractive, to represent them. Oprah didn't consider herself a beauty and still doesn't. But to her surprise, she won the contest and became the first African American to carry the title of Miss Fire Prevention.

High school graduation soon followed, and Oprah continued her job as the "voice of WVOL" through the summer. Despite

❋

At 16, Oprah won a speech contest sponsored by the Elks Club. The prize was a full scholarship to Tennessee State University.

During the late 1960s and early 1970s, Oprah's talent for public speaking and broadcasting began to blossom. At age 16, she won a full scholarship to Tennessee State University.

the scholarship she'd won to Tennessee State, Oprah felt a strong desire to get away from Nashville and her ever-watchful father. But Vernon wouldn't hear of it. So, in the fall she entered the freshman class of all-black TSU. It would not be a high point of her young life. This was the early 1970s, when student radicalism and the black-power movement were at their height. Young black students were supposed to be angry, anti-establishment, and political. Independent-minded Oprah didn't fit in.

"I hated, hated, hated college," she told
People magazine. ". . . Everybody was angry
for four years. . . . I never felt the kind of
repression other black people are expected
to. I think I was called 'nigger' once, when
I was in fifth grade."

Her classmates called her an "Uncle
Tom" and shunned her. In her freshman
year, while other students were protesting
and staging sit-ins, Oprah dared to do the
unthinkable—she entered more beauty
pageants. She saw these contests as a way
to show off her talents as a speech and
drama major. If she won, she could earn
some money to pay for her education, too.

Although the beauty contests she entered
were for African-American women, Oprah
already felt she had one strike against her.
"I was raised to believe that the lighter your
skin, the better you were," she told _Ms._
magazine. "I wasn't light-skinned, so I
decided to be the best and the smartest."

During the Miss Black Nashville pageant,
Oprah was asked what she wanted to do
with her life. She had prepared to say that
she wanted to be an elementary school
teacher. However, on the morning of the
interview, she happened to turn on the
Today Show and see Barbara Walters, one
of her heroes. When the time came to

answer the question, she told the judges, "I believe in truth, and I want to perpetuate truth. So I want to be a journalist." She won the pageant.

Three months later, Oprah went on to represent Nashville in the first Miss Black Tennessee pageant. She shocked herself and many other people as well by winning "on poise and talent." She won another scholarship and flew to Hollywood to represent the state of Tennessee in the Miss Black America pageant.

Oprah went into the competition with high marks, but refused to make herself glamorous for the judges. Her chaperon, or companion, at the pageant remains convinced that if Oprah had made more of an effort to fit the beauty-queen role, she would have won. As it turned out, she wasn't even a finalist.

From Radio to Television

Instead, Oprah got what turned out to be the career opportunity of a lifetime. A person from the local CBS-TV station in Nashville, WTVF, caught her act in the pageant and asked her to audition for a job as the station's first African-American news anchorperson. Surprisingly, Oprah was reluctant to accept. She was afraid that if

One of Oprah's earliest inspirations to enter broadcasting came from Barbara Walters. Here, Oprah poses with her idol backstage at a journalism-awards ceremony.

she got the job it would interfere with her college work. Oprah's speech teacher, however, finally convinced her that she shouldn't turn down such a golden opportunity. She auditioned and got the job. At the time, TV stations across the country were searching for women and minorities to hire. "Sure I was a token," Oprah readily admitted years later. "But honey, I was one happy token."

Oprah was so well received on the weekend news that she was quickly promoted to the nightly news. Her boss and mentor, news director Chris Clark, knew Oprah was made for television broadcasting. "Her emotions came right out there," he said. "That's what made her so good."

Although not radical, Oprah wasn't afraid to stand up to racism and bigotry when she encountered it. During one assignment, a bigoted shop owner in a segregated white neighborhood refused to shake her hand. He remarked, "We don't shake hands with niggers down here." Oprah smiled and said, "I'll bet the niggers are glad."

At 22, Oprah was a rising star in the local media. But she was still living at home under her father's strict rules. She was, she now says, "the only news anchor in the country who had to be home by midnight."

When a job offer came from ABC-TV station WJZ in Baltimore, Maryland, Oprah jumped at it. Her decision had as much to do with getting out of the family nest as it did with furthering her career. She deeply loved her father, but she was now an adult and needed to be on her own.

"She knew the door was open to come back," recalls Chris Clark. "But she was in the big time now."

Chapter 3

Lost and Found in TV Land

WJZ-TV in Baltimore looked like the answer to all Oprah's dreams. She would be co-anchoring the six o'clock news in the tenth largest city in America. Her co-anchor would be the dean of Baltimore newscasters, Jerry Turner. She would be earning a six-figure salary. She would be famous. All over Baltimore, billboards were going up announcing her arrival and asking the provocative question, "What's an Oprah?" The answer to that question, however, did not please the management at WJZ.

A Square Peg in a Round Hole

In a major city like Baltimore, newscasters were expected to maintain a professional style that went against the grain of Oprah's personality. Big-time anchors delivered the news straight, with as little editorial comment as possible. They read through the

Oprah has always had a strong sense of personal identity. During her early years in broadcasting, her style, appearance, and dress were somewhat unique among her colleagues. Here, Oprah relaxes with friends at the Hippo restaurant in Chicago.

news copy several times before airtime to make sure that they pronounced every word correctly and that there were no factual mistakes in the writing.

Oprah refused to do this. She wanted to be spontaneous and fresh every night. She wouldn't look at the copy until she was on the air, getting the news at the same time as viewers. But, unfortunately, this style led to some terrible flubs. The worst one was when Oprah mispronounced *Canada.* It was such a silly mistake that she laughed out loud at herself. So much for the professional dignity WJZ was looking for!

But the incident revealed something to Oprah. "It was the first time I had shown any resemblance to truth on the air," she said later. "Before that, I was a twinkle doll . . . I was *pretending* to be something. I wasn't real."

Oprah's decision to be herself led to other problems. TV reporters, like other journalists, are supposed to be objective and distance themselves from the news they are announcing. Oprah had great difficulty with this. On one occasion, she was sent to interview a woman whose seven children had perished in a fire. Oprah felt she couldn't invade this woman's privacy during her grief, and she returned to the station to tell her boss. He told her to go back to interview the woman, or he would fire her. Oprah tried again and ended up weeping on the taped segment along with the grieving woman. When the tape ran on the newscast, Oprah apologized to the TV audience for not maintaining more professionalism.

The apology may have satisfied viewers, but it didn't work with the station management. On April 1, 1977, Oprah was told that she was being relieved of her duties on the six o'clock news. It was a terrible blow at the time, but Oprah today realizes that her bosses were right. "I had no business anchoring the news in a major market.... I was only twenty-two."

Still, Oprah had a long-term contract with WJZ, and the station was stuck with her. The question was, how were they going to use her? For the time being, Oprah was demoted to broadcasting the early morning local news updates during ABC's popular morning talk show, *Good Morning, America.*

It wasn't just her professionalism that was bad, management decided; it was also her personal appearance. One day the assistant news director sat her down and delivered the news. "Your hair's too long. It's too thick. Your eyes are too far apart. Your nose is too wide. Your chin is too wide. And you need to do something about it."

The former Miss Black Tennessee was distressed—she didn't think she was so unattractive. But to keep her job, Oprah dutifully agreed to let the station send her to a fancy French hairstyling salon in New York City. The stylists made her feel like a helpless guinea pig. With strong chemical lotion, they thinned and permed her hair.

✳

"I had no business anchoring the news in a major market.... I was only twenty-two."

"I felt the lotion burning my skull," Oprah recalls. "I kept telling them, 'Excuse me, this is beginning to burn a little.' Hell, it wasn't burning—it was *flaming*."

Soon after she returned to Baltimore, Oprah's hair began to fall out. Within a week she was completely bald. "They tried to change me, and then they're stuck with a bald, black anchorwoman," she said. Unable to find a wig to fit her head, Oprah was forced to wear brightly colored scarves to hide her baldness. It was a horrible experience, but Oprah's ability to laugh at herself helped her to get through it.

WJZ management, however, had not quite finished with the "new" Oprah idea yet. If they couldn't do anything with her appearance, they would try to improve her speech. Again, this was odd, since Oprah's voice and speech were seen as her greatest assets in her previous broadcasting jobs. But the people at WJZ said she sounded "too nice" and sent her back to New York, this time to a speech coach who could "toughen her up."

The speech coach could find nothing wrong with Oprah's on-air delivery. Instead, she coached Oprah to stand up to the management and not let them boss her around. But Oprah was much "too nice" to follow this advice very far. It's a problem she admits she still has in most of her relationships today.

A New Start

Then something happened that changed the direction of Oprah's career. A new station manager began developing a local morning talk show to compete with the extremely popular *Phil Donahue Show,* which was aired on another Baltimore station. Donahue's candid, outspoken style had made him the number-one host of daytime talk shows. The local show WJZ ran against Donahue was called *People Are Talking.* Oprah was picked to be its new co-host, opposite popular WJZ personality Richard Sher.

Oprah wasn't thrilled to get the job. She had struck out as a newscaster and now saw herself being demoted once again to a lower rung on the station's ladder. If this job didn't work out, she thought to herself, WJZ might find a way to get rid of her entirely.

But on her very first day of *People Are Talking,* Oprah made a valuable discovery about herself. She felt very much at home interviewing guests on the show. And she didn't need to be objective or distant either. She could laugh and joke and just be herself. When the show ended, Oprah thought, "This is what I was born to do. This is like breathing."

Viewers agreed. Oprah was a natural when it came to talking to people. She avoided using a script or using prepared questions, just as she had on the news. This time being spontaneous worked. Oprah asked questions of celebrities that viewers themselves would have liked to ask. Although she had fun on the show, she also took it seriously. She cared about people, and this came through in every interview she did.

"There was this way she had of looking at you," recalled a frequent guest, entertainment writer Dick Maurice, "and you felt that, when you were talking to her, the only person she was thinking about was you. It was a look in her eyes. You could see a soul there."

The ratings for *People Are Talking* took off, and the show quickly knocked Phil Donahue from his number-one position in the time slot. But while Oprah's career was soaring, her personal life was in a tailspin.

For four years she was in a destructive relationship with a man who mentally and verbally abused her. It was a familiar and

✳

Oprah was a natural when it came to talking to people. She avoided using a script or using prepared questions, just as she had on the news.

frightening pattern. The guilt and worthlessness she felt as an abused teenager had remained and continued to affect her adult relationships with men. Feeling unworthy of love, Oprah often seemed to be attracted to men who would hurt her. "The more he rejected me, the more I wanted him," she has commented about their affair. "I felt depleted, powerless."

One day her boyfriend told her he was leaving her for good. Oprah didn't believe him at first, but as weeks passed without a phone call, she began to feel more and more depressed. Finally, she wrote a long suicide note to her best friend. Depressed as she was about the breakup, Oprah now says that she never could have done anything. Despite the pain, she just had too much to live for.

Chicago Beckons

Oprah was ready for a change—not just in her personal relationships, but in her career, too. As much as she had enjoyed her six years with Richard Sher on *People Are Talking*, Oprah was anxious to host a show on her own. "I really grew up there in Baltimore, you understand," she says today. "I felt natural and cared for there. But it was time to move on."

(*Opposite page*)
During the early 1980s, Oprah's success in the talkshow market began to take off. In 1983, she decided to leave her show in Baltimore for *A.M. Chicago*.

Oprah got her opportunity to move through her show's associate producer, Debbie DiMaio. Like Oprah, Debbie had wanted to be on her own. Debbie had taken a job as a full producer at WLS-TV in Chicago, Illinois, and decided to give Oprah's audition tape to the producers of the morning talk show, *A.M. Chicago.* Needless to say, the producers were greatly impressed and invited Oprah to Chicago. Oprah wasn't sure that she would like Chicago and was uncertain about the job move. But when she arrived there on September 4, 1983, to meet the station executives, everything changed. ". . . I set foot in this city, and just walking down the street, it was like roots, like the motherland," she recalls. "I knew I belonged here." The toast of Baltimore was on her way to superstardom in the Windy City.

Chapter 4

Hitting the Big Time

Before Oprah's arrival, *A.M. Chicago* had been just another lightweight morning talk show, with, as Oprah puts it, a heavy emphasis, on "mascara and cooking." All that changed with Oprah. She wanted to make people think as they drank their second cup of morning coffee—she also wanted to entertain them. Her guests included not only a popular lineup of Hollywood celebrities, but also people with true-to-life stories to tell—the physically challenged, the divorced, people with a cause. Some of her guests were controversial. On one show she had a group of white racists. Unlike some talk-show hosts, Oprah didn't condemn these people. "I don't try to change people," she later said. "I try to expose them for what they are."

A Feeling Person

Phil Donahue had been featuring these kinds of controversial guests for years, but Oprah's approach was quite original. As one perceptive TV critic pointed out, Phil Donahue's approach to the problems he discusses is intellectual rather than emotional, whereas "Oprah feels them—if she hasn't outright lived them."

Oprah's caring way with her guests was striking. Most talk-show hosts sat behind a desk or at a safe distance from their guests in an easy chair. Oprah leaned in close from her chair, determined to hear every word her guests spoke. If she felt particularly moved, she would reach out and hold a person's hand. There was nothing fake or planned about Oprah. She was always herself—spontaneous, caring, supportive, and vulnerable. Audience's responded strongly to her sincerity.

Another side of Oprah's personality that attracted viewers to her show was her unpredictability. "When Oprah got her own show, it was bringing a child to an open schoolroom," recalls her longtime friend and producer, Debbie DiMaio. "For Oprah it was, 'Here's your chance to do it. Ask any question you've ever wanted to ask, when you want to ask it.'"

Never working from a prepared list of questions, Oprah asked only the questions that came up during the conversation. With celebrities, she skipped over the usual career questions and tried to find out who the person behind the name was. Oprah's methods often led to startling but moving discoveries about people. While many guests found her interviews refreshing, many were nervous about what she might ask. When the African-American leader Reverend Jesse Jackson came on her show, Oprah asked him if he had been nervous meeting the former Russian leader Mikhail Gorbachev. Jackson, who usually appears quite cool and confident, replied, "I was

Oprah has tackled many tough issues on her show. Here, she speaks with the audience during a show on racial segregation in Cumming, Georgia.

Despite her hectic schedule, Oprah still works tirelessly to aid those less fortunate than she. In 1986, she worked to promote HandsAcrossAmerica, a nationwide effort to raise money to fight poverty.

more nervous when I met you. You're more unpredictable."

There were times, however, when Oprah herself was nervous. During one show, Oprah interviewed a group of nudists. While the studio audience saw the guests naked, cameras showed only the nudists' faces to the TV audience. For Oprah, the show was distressing, if not slightly comical. "I had to act like it was a perfectly normal thing to be interviewing a bunch of naked people and not look," she said.

Oprah also admits that she has a hard time interviewing people for whom she has great admiration. She either becomes too eager to please and starstruck, or she gets tongue-tied. This happened both with Barbara Walters, her inspiration, and Maya Angelou, one of her favorite writers. One role model who did not appear on her show was her crosstown competitor, Phil Donahue. She watched Donahue's show regularly for some time, but finally had to stop because she found herself trying to imitate him.

Driving Out the Competition

Chicago found Oprah Winfrey to be a true original in the tired world of TV talk shows. By February 1984, after she had been on the air for just one month, *A.M. Chicago* had its highest ratings in years, with one fourth of the entire TV audience tuning in. This put Oprah's *A.M. Chicago* ahead of Donahue's show in Chicago. Oprah, with her fresh approach and appealing style, was beating Donahue, who, for more than 16 years, had been unchallenged in his time slot. The station bosses at WLS knew that they had a new star on their hands, and they acted accordingly. *A.M. Chicago* was expanded from 30 minutes to one full

hour and at the same time was renamed
The Oprah Winfrey Show.

As Oprah celebrated her first anniversary
in Chicago, Phil Donahue announced he
was moving his show to New York City. The
reason he gave for the move was to be with
his wife, the actress Marlo Thomas, who
spent much of the year in New York. Many
viewers, however, felt that Oprah's success
was the real reason behind Donahue's
move. Oprah herself did not believe this
and still has the "highest respect" for her
foremost competitor. "I learned how to
do what I do because of him," she has said.
At a farewell luncheon, Donahue said he
wished Oprah well, but "just not in [his]
time slot."

But if Phil thought their rivalry was over,
he was sadly mistaken. Oprah and her
business manager, Jeff Jacobs, had already
put together a syndication deal by June of
1985. Syndication would allow them to sell
the show to TV stations all across the country. Oprah's success with her local show
in Chicago had already drawn national
attention. *Newsweek* magazine had done
a full-page story on her. And she had
appeared as a guest on NBC's *Tonight Show,*
where she had talked about her weight
problem with a sympathetic Joan Rivers.

Into Syndication

A number of TV syndicators had flocked to broadcast Oprah's show nationwide. King World Productions, the syndicators of such successful game shows as *The Wheel of Fortune* and *Jeopardy*, offered her a deal too good to refuse. Oprah would receive a large share of the gross profits from the show—the largest to date for a talk-show host. When 137 local stations across the country signed up for *The Oprah Winfrey Show*, another record was broken.

Oprah stands with television executives after announcing the syndication of *A.M. Chicago.* Before syndication, the show was renamed *The Oprah Winfrey Show.*

✳

Within just three months, The Oprah Winfrey Show *was rated number one in its time slot.*

On September 8, 1986, the syndicated daytime show premiered nationwide. The first program was predictably offbeat. Its featured guests were an author of a book on how to get a mate and several people who paid $95 for the book. The show's first reviews were mixed. One critic found Oprah to be a Donahue "imposter." But another critic praised her for her "down-home, almost funky style," concluding, "Oprah isn't so full of herself that she'll avoid asking the questions most viewers would like to ask."

Within just three months, *The Oprah Winfrey Show* was rated number one in its time slot in the Nielsen ratings, which are based on polls of TV viewers. This wasn't bad for the first national TV talk show hosted by an African-American woman. Oprah was not only a national TV star now, but she was also very rich. By the summer of 1987 she had moved into a luxury apartment in Chicago's exclusive lakefront area and had already become a millionaire by the age of 32. But there were many things that were more important to her than financial success. One of these things had nothing to do with being the host of America's number-one talk show.

Chapter 5

Oprah the Actress

Acting was Oprah Winfrey's first ambition. All through elementary and high school, Oprah earned praise for her outstanding dramatic readings. When she arrived at Tennessee State University, she took the advice of her theater professor and majored in speech and drama. Due to her busy schedule, however, Oprah performed in only one full-length play. She portrayed Coretta King, wife of the late Dr. Martin Luther King. Oprah later came in second at a Chicago drama conference with a stirring reading from Ntozake Shange's play *For Colored Girls Who Have Considered Suicide/When the Rainbow is Enuf.*

A Dream Role

Once she left college to pursue her broadcasting career, Oprah's aspirations to act went on hold. Then, in 1985, after she had started working in Chicago, things changed. Musician and producer Quincy Jones had come to Chicago to testify at a hearing for singer Michael Jackson over rights for a song Jackson had written. While relaxing in his hotel room, Jones flipped on the television and happened to catch Oprah on *A.M. Chicago.* Oprah's warmth and honesty impressed him. He thought Oprah would be perfect for a role in his new movie, *The Color Purple,* based on Alice Walker's novel. Jones called the film's casting director to set up an audition for her.

Oprah couldn't believe her good fortune. *The Color Purple* was one of her favorite books, and she had already known the movie was being planned. "I would have been [anything]. Script girl. Xerox person," she later said. "I would do whatever. It had not occurred to me that maybe I could have a role in it."

The part she tried out for was Sofia, the best friend of the heroine, Celie. Oprah was nervous at the audition. For one thing, she had come down with the flu. For another, the director of the picture was Steven Spielberg, one of Hollywood's top directors and the man who had made the hit movie *E.T.* She didn't have to worry.

(*Opposite page*)
In 1987, Oprah received the Golden Apple trophy from the Hollywood Women's Press Club for her outstanding work in broadcasting.

In 1985, Oprah portrayed Sofia in the film version of Alice Walker's *The Color Purple* and received an Academy Award nomination for her performance.

Spielberg loved her screen test, and she got the part. Oprah calls it "the greatest moment in my life. . . . Maybe the day I was born was greater, but I can't remember that experience."

The motion picture was an unusual one for Spielberg, who was best known for his fantasy and adventure movies. *The Color Purple* was a realistic drama about African Americans in the South during the early 1900s. Celie, the heroine, was a poor black girl struggling against white racism and the brutality of her black husband. Celie was played by Whoopi Goldberg, who was then known only as a comedian.

The Color Purple was shot on location in Monroe, North Carolina. Oprah now says that if her bosses at WLS hadn't given her the time off to do the movie, she would have quit her job. Oprah recalls the three months she worked on the film as "the one time in my life I experienced total harmony."

Like Celie, Sofia suffers terribly. She is beaten and imprisoned by whites for being an "uppity" black woman. But her spirit is never destroyed. Oprah had known many women like Sofia and Celie. She understood them. "Sofia teaches us that there is a great will and power inside us all, and that you can overcome anything," she says. "You can be down, you can even be broken, but there's always a way to mend."

Oscar Agony

When *The Color Purple* was released in December 1985, Chicago film critic Gene Siskel described Oprah's performance as "shockingly good." The film was nominated for 11 Academy Awards. And both Whoopi and Oprah were recognized—Whoopi as best actress and Oprah as best actress in a supporting role. Oprah, who had never acted in a film before, was being singled out for one of the best performances of the year. It was an amazing experience.

Oprah looked forward to the night the Oscar trophies would be awarded. She planned to wear a new dress, specially designed for her. But only a few hours before the ceremonies were to begin, she discovered the dress didn't fit. With the help of three friends, Oprah managed to squeeze into the "killer dress." But it was just the beginning of her troubles.

"[W]hen I tried to sit down, the collar rode up and choked me," she wrote in *Ebony* magazine. "I wound up riding to the Oscars flat on my back in the back of a limousine. I asked the driver to let me out a block away so people wouldn't see me trying to get out of the car. Sitting in the theater was even worse. I had to pull the collar down and straighten my back every time I had to get up and sit back down. . . . Right before the category of best supporting actress was to be announced . . . I heard the voice of God. 'You are not going to win this award!' He said, 'because you cannot get up to accept it!'"

To Oprah's great relief, Angelica Huston won. Aside from her dress, Oprah felt that she "hadn't paid enough acting dues" to win an Oscar. She was disappointed, however, that *The Color Purple* didn't get any awards at all.

(*Opposite page*)
Oprah takes a minute to pose before the press at the 1987 Academy Awards ceremony.

Oscar or no Oscar, Oprah had now been bitten by the acting bug. She was quickly cast in another screen version of a serious novel dealing with the African-American experience—Richard Wright's *Native Son.* This book tells the story of Bigger Thomas, a young African-American man growing up in the streets of Chicago during the 1930s. Through a series of circumstances, Bigger Thomas accidentally kills a rich, young white girl.

Oprah was cast as Bigger's mother. While it was a small role, it was a touching one. Unfortunately, the film was not a great success. Oprah had artistic differences with the director. And the film eventually proved to be a commercial failure. Some critics found Oprah's performance too sentimental. She modeled the role after her own mother and the difficulties she had in raising Oprah.

After *Native Son,* Oprah decided that she wanted to produce shows and movies in addition to acting in them. She bought a 100,000-square-foot-TV-and-production studio in August of 1988 and established Harpo Incorporated. Harpo, which is "Oprah" spelled backward, would allow Oprah to produce films that had "social importance" and that appealed to her

✳

After Native Son, *Oprah decided that she wanted to produce shows and movies in addition to acting in them.*

personally. Oprah had now realized yet another dream. She was the first African American, and only the third woman, to own a major TV-and-film-production studio.

Acting on Television

It wasn't long before Harpo found its first film project. Oprah read the novel *The Women of Brewster Place* by Gloria Naylor and fell in love with it. It was the story of seven African-American women living in a tenement building who struggle to survive in the inner city. It was a tough subject to sell to a movie studio, but Oprah thought it would make a great TV miniseries. All three major networks, however, disagreed. Still, Oprah was determined to see *The Women of Brewster Place* produced. She gave copies of the novel to ABC executives, urging them to read it and reconsider. They did, and within days Oprah was signed on to act in and produce her own four-hour miniseries.

The cast of *The Women of Brewster Place* included such notable African-American actors as Cicely Tyson, Paul Winfield, and Robin Givens. Oprah played Mattie Michaels, a woman who loses everything she holds dear when her son gets into trouble with the law. To prepare for the

At the NAACP Image Awards in 1989, Oprah received numerous honors for her work as an actress, a producer, and a talk-show host.

Oprah starred in and produced the successful miniseries *The Women of Brewster Place.* The program, which aired in 1989, was such a hit that ABC offered to make it into a series.

role, Oprah kept a 200-page journal of the feelings she thought Mattie might have had. She created an entire life for her.

The Women of Brewster Place was so successful that ABC offered Oprah a weekly series based on the characters. Against all the advice of her closest friends, Oprah seized the opportunity and rushed the series into production. "I could hear my inner voice telling me it wasn't time, don't do it . . . but I thought I could make it all right because I wanted it to be all right."

Producing a weekly TV series while doing a talk show five nights a week proved to be exhausting. "I was working around the clock," Oprah recalls. "We'd leave here [the studio] at two in the morning and come back at six to do the show."

The results were not up to Oprah's high standards. *Brewster Place*, which first aired in 1990, received low ratings and was canceled after 10 weeks. "I felt relief," Oprah said. Besides, Oprah's daytime talk show was still setting records. And it was making her one of the wealthiest people in the world of entertainment.

Chapter 6

A Real Person in a Fake World

On September 8, 1991, Oprah marked five years as a nationally syndicated talk-show host. It was certainly an occasion to celebrate. *The Oprah Winfrey Show* was by then one of the highest-rated daytime programs in television history. In May of 1993, Oprah won her fourth daytime Emmy—her third one in a row. More than 20 million viewers tuned in each day. Oprah's earnings were estimated at $40 million a year, which made her the highest-paid performer in show business. She had already signed a contract that assured her the show would continue through 1994–1995.

Formula for Success

What makes Oprah's show such a success? Perhaps TV critic Marvin Kitman put it best when he wrote that Oprah is "a real person in the fake world of TV." Oprah's

Oprah's frankness and sincerity have made her one of the most popular talk-show hosts on television.

(*Opposite page*)
Over the years, Oprah and her show have received many honors and awards, including the daytime Emmy for three straight years: 1991, 1992, and 1993. Here, the daytime superstar stands with one of her Emmys in 1991.

"realness" goes far beyond being friendly, frank, and sympathetic. Other talk-show hosts have a good ability to identify with people's problems, but Oprah admits to her own, as that famous program on incest made clear. Since her disclosure, Oprah has talked about her experiences as an abused child and troubled teenager, hoping to educate the public and help people in similar situations.

The 1991 brutal murder of a four-year-old Chicago girl by a convicted child abuser moved Oprah to testify in front of the U.S. Senate. With the help of former Illinois governor James Thompson, she drafted a federal child protection bill that proposed

Oprah has always tried to remain active in social causes. Here, she lends a helping hand at a Habitat for Humanity project that builds shelters in Chicago.

the creation of a national data bank, with the names of convicted sex offenders. It would particularly target those who have committed crimes against children. Oprah hoped the data bank would allow schools and child-care centers across the country to screen potential job applicants and current employees with their consent.

For the Senate Judiciary Committee, Oprah recalled her own experience with child abuse and the horror she felt after hearing of the circumstances that surrounded the murder. "I wept for Angelica [the murdered girl]," she said. "And I wept for us, a society that apparently cares so little about its children that we would allow a man with two previous convictions for kidnapping and rape of children to go free after serving only seven years of a fifteen-year sentence."

Just as Oprah has shared her life to help others, she has also shared her wealth. Friends praise her for her generosity. Oprah has given co-workers and relatives fur coats, money, and all-expense-paid vacations. When seven members of her staff were turned down for raises from the station boss, Oprah gave each of them $10,000 in cash that she had stuffed inside rolls of toilet paper.

"Material success is rewarding and a lot of fun, but it's not the most important thing in my life," she says. "...I know when this is *all* over, the Master isn't going to ask me how many things I owned or how many television shows I did. I think the questions will be, 'What did I do to make a difference? Did I learn to live with love in my heart?'"

Oprah has given millions of dollars and much of her time to good causes, including a million-dollar donation she made to Morehouse College, an all-black men's college in Atlanta, Georgia. She has given scholarships to students at Tennessee State University and used to spend two Saturdays a month working with underprivileged African-American girls who live in Chicago's Cabrini-Green housing project.

In the 1980s, Oprah dedicated much of her time to the Cabrini-Green housing project in Chicago. In 1985, she spoke to residents about attaining success.

Oprah and actress Cybill Shepherd hold up their People's Choice Awards in 1988. Oprah was voted favorite talk-show host on television.

As if this were not enough, Oprah spends a great deal of time lecturing at various homeless shelters, youth groups, and churches about such issues as child abuse and education. Nobody who comes to her with a problem is turned away. When a woman on the verge of suicide called her, Oprah stayed on the line with her for two hours. After the crisis, Oprah paid for her psychiatric treatment.

Oprah views her hour on the air each day as much more than entertainment. "In a profound yet subtle way, it is a ministry," she has commented. "It does what a ministry should do: uplift people, encourage them and give them a sense of hope about themselves."

Facing Personal Challenges

Much as Oprah has been able to help others, she hasn't been able to always solve her own problems. One problem has been her struggle with her weight. She began overeating during her uneasy days at WJZ in Baltimore. "Eating is a drug for me," she confesses. "It's what I do when I'm really happy, and it's what I do when I'm tired. It's what I do when I'm not sure if I'm happy or tired. It is a disease."

To lick the disease and shed unwanted pounds, Oprah has gone on a variety of diets. In 1988, she seemed to have finally conquered fat. She came on the show one day proudly pulling a wagon loaded with 67 pounds of lard—the weight she had lost. She was thin and seemed determined to stay that way. But in two years, Oprah had gained back every pound. Sick of the struggle, she vowed never to go on another diet. Since then, she seems to have come to terms with her weight, accepting herself for who she is, which most of her fans did a long time ago.

In Chicago, Oprah's usual struggle with romantic relationships continued. Even though things were better than they had been in Baltimore, her love life remained unstable. Oprah, with her rich sense of

*

Oprah spends a great deal of time lecturing at various homeless shelters, youth groups, and churches.... Nobody who comes to her with a problem is turned away.

humor, joked to viewers that "Mr. Right" was on his way but was "in Africa, walking." In fact, he was a lot closer.

(*Opposite page*) Oprah shows off her new, slim figure to a studio audience after having lost 67 pounds through diet and exercise in 1988.

"Mr. Right" Appears

At the many social functions that she attended in Chicago, Oprah kept running into a tall, extremely good-looking former model and basketball player, Stedman Graham. Stedman cofounded Athletes

Oprah and longtime boyfriend Stedman Graham were engaged in November 1992.

Against Drugs, a nonprofit organization, and now runs his own public relations firm. One day he asked Oprah out, but she was in awe of his good looks, and turned him down. He persisted, and she kept saying no. Oprah later admitted that she had a hard time believing Stedman was actually seriously interested in her. Finally, after she had a particularly bad day at work, Oprah agreed to a date. Their first night out together was a revelation. Oprah later told her friends at the studio that Stedman "bought me roses, paid for dinner, and was interested in what I had to say!" In only a short time, their growing relationship turned into a serious and steady romance.

Oprah refers to "Steddie" as "the best man who's ever been in my life" and "my rock." She says, "When I'm going through a grinning and gripping festival, shaking hands and smiling and I'm ready to scream that I can't take it anymore, I'll look over at Stedman standing in the corner and see him saying, 'Yeah, you can do it.'"

Oprah and Stedman have been together for more than seven years, and in November of 1992, they were engaged at Oprah's farmhouse in Indiana. Oprah's fans began eagerly awaiting news of wedding plans.

Television ratings soared as millions of American viewers tuned in to watch Oprah interview superstar Michael Jackson on February 10, 1993. Media-shy Jackson opened up to Oprah as he took her on a tour of his estate in Santa Ynez, California.

What Next?

Oprah was not involved in much acting or producing after *Brewster Place* went off the air. During that time, Harpo's studio was mostly used for the production of *The Oprah Winfrey Show* and was rented for making television commercials.

During these years, however, Oprah developed some new film and television projects that she was interested in. Some of these projects were based on books for which she owns the film rights, such as Toni Morrison's Pulitzer Prize-winning novel *Beloved*, and Alex Kantrowitz's *There Are No Children Here* (which started production in the summer of 1993 for ABC).

Where Oprah will go from here is anyone's guess. She has already proved her abilities in many ways—by acting, by producing, and by interviewing. And despite her fame and success, she has also proved that she still places the highest value on honesty, compassion, and positive personal growth. "I still want what I've always wanted," Oprah has said. "I used to write it in my diaries when I was 15 years old, and I'm still writing it and saying it all the time: 'I just want to be the best person I can be.' That part of me hasn't changed and that's the *who* of who I am to me."

"I just want to be the best person I can be. That part of me hasn't changed and that's the who of who I am to me."

Glossary
Explaining New Words

anchorperson A person who coordinates and reads reports from correspondents on a television news program.

audition A tryout for a singer, an actor, or other performer.

critic A writer or commentator who gives opinions on new books, plays, films, television shows, or the other arts.

disc jockey A radio announcer whose program consists mostly of recorded music.

miniseries A dramatic TV special that is shown in parts over several evenings.

news copy The written script that a radio or TV anchorperson or correspondent reads on the air.

news director The person who runs the news department of a radio or TV station.

Nielsen ratings A rating system that determines the number of viewers watching a television program.

Oscars The informal name for the statuettes given yearly by the Motion Picture Academy of Arts and Sciences; also known as Academy Awards.

producer A person in charge of putting together a television show or film.

production company An organization capable of producing its own television programs or films.

screen test The filmed audition of an actor to see how he or she looks and sounds on film.

station manager The person who oversees the operation of a TV or radio station.

studio A building where films or TV shows are produced.

studio audience A group of people who see a television program as it is taped live in the studio.

syndicated show A TV program that is produced independently and sold to individual stations around the country.

time slot The time each day or week that a TV program is regularly seen.

For Further Reading

Beaton, Margaret. *Oprah Winfrey: TV Talk Show Host.* Chicago, IL: Childrens Press, 1990.

Koral, April. *In the Newsroom.* New York: Franklin Watts, 1990.

Malone, Mary. *Barbara Walters: T.V. Superstar.* Hillside, NJ: Enslow Publishers, 1990.

Morrison, Toni. *Beloved.* New York: Alfred Knopf, 1987.

Patterson, Lillie, and Wright, Cornelia H. *Oprah Winfrey: Talk Show Host & Actress.* Hillside, NJ: Enslow Publishers, 1990.

Saidman, Anne. *Oprah Winfrey: Media Success Story.* Minneapolis, MN: Lerner Publications, 1990.

Walker, Alice. *The Color Purple.* San Diego, CA: Harcourt Brace Jovanovich, 1982.

Woods, Geraldine. *Oprah Winfrey.* New York: Macmillan Children's Book Group, 1991.

Wright, Richard. *Native Son.* New York: HarperCollins, 1969.

Index